W9-AYE-724

Amtrak*ing*

A Guide to Enjoyable Train Travel

by Mauris L. Emeka

Apollo Publishing Company
Port Orchard, Washington 98366

Apollo Publishing Company
Box 1937
Port Orchard, Washington 98366-0805

Publisher's Cataloging in Publication

Emeka, Mauris L.
    AMTRAK*ing*: a guide to enjoyable train travel /
    by Mauris L. Emeka.
    p. cm
    Rev. ed. of: Getting the most from rail travel.
    Includes index.
    Preassigned LCCN: 93-90727.
    ISBN 0-9640125-0-2
    1. Railroad travel—United States—Guidebooks.
    2. Railroad travel—United States—History.
    3. Railroads—United States—
    Vocational guidance. I. Emeka, Mauris L.
    Getting the most from rail travel. II. Title.

HE2727.E44 1994   385'.0973
                                         QBI94-94

Printed in the U.S.A. on acid-free 50% recycled Paper

. . . Dedicated to those who truly love the magic of riding the rails.

A distinctive advantage of train travel—a "see-level" view of the country.

Courtesy of National
Railroad Passenger Corp.

About the Author

M auris L. Emeka is a writer who has enjoyed train travel since his childhood days in Wynne, Arkansas, and Abilene, Texas. He has been employed as an Amtrak train attendant since 1989.

This is Mr. Emeka's third published book, his second on the subject of trains. He finished college at the University of Kansas, and graduated with an MBA from the University of Washington. Married and the father of four children, Mr. Emeka lives in Port Orchard, Washington.

Acknowledgements

To my wife, Sunday, for her untiring efforts in proofreading and critiquing the original manuscript. I deeply appreciate that she can cut through the verbiage and get right to the heart of an idea.

To passengers and fellow train crew members for encouraging me to undertake the writing of this book.

Special thanks to Bob Anderson of Palmer Lake, Colorado, for allowing parts of his book entitled "Stretching" to be used in Chapter 9.

I am grateful to Jeff Schultz of Olympia, Washington for the cover photo of an Amtrak train with the Tacoma Narrows Bridge in the background.

Special thanks to Dorothy Kavka and her staff at Evanston Publishing Co. (Evanston, IL) for their timely and invaluable services in helping make this book a reality.

Last but certainly not least, I thank Debra Munn of Amarillo, Texas for her patience and thoroughness in proofreading and editing the final draft of the manuscript.

Foreword

Rail passenger service in this country has come a long way from its near death almost twenty-five years ago. When Congress created Amtrak, many thought the passenger train would quickly die, the victim of competition from freeways and jet airplanes. However, Amtrak acquired new equipment, completed major capital improvements projects, and most important, rejuvenated interest and ridership in passenger trains. Clearly, the passenger train is here to stay.

In the United States, policy makers have been looking at the passenger train as one important component in enhancing our mobility. In many locations across the country, highways are choked by gridlock and our airports by winglock. Furthermore, our cities fail to meet air quality standards in many locations due to automobile emissions. Dependable, frequent, and convenient intercity rail passenger service is one cost-effective alternative to provide mobility for our citizens, reduce our dependence on imported petroleum, and help reduce air pollution.

Here in the state of Washington, we are working to establish a new high speed rail corridor through incremental improvements to existing railroad tracks. The Pacific Northwest Rail corridor is an example of private/public partnership with the Washington State Department of Transportation, the Oregon Department of Transportation, the Province of British Columbia, Burlington Northern Railroad, Southern Pacific Railroad, Amtrak, and other organizations all cooperating to realize the goal of frequent rail passenger service between Vancouver, British Columbia; Seattle, Washington; and Eugene, Oregon. Our commitment is to provide high quality rail passenger service along the Pacific Northwest Rail Corridor.

This book is a handy companion for anyone thinking about taking a train trip. Throughout this book, the reader will find clear and concise information and tips about rail travel. Many people have not been on a train at all or for many years. This book is written especially for them. But whether you are a novice or an experienced train traveler, this book will help you get the most from your next Amtrak journey.

Sid Morrison
Secretary of Transportation
Washington State Department of
Transportation

February 1, 1994

CONTENTS

About the Author v

Acknowledgements vi

Foreword vii

Introduction xiii

Chapter 1
The Magic of A Train 1

Chapter 2
A Brief History of Passenger Trains . . 5
   The early years 5
   1860 and after 7
   Motor cars replace trains 10
   Amtrak is launched 11

Chapter 3
What's Available —
Equipment and Services 13
   Coach cars 13
   Sleeper car accommodations 17
   Dining car and lounge car 20
   Services for senior citizens and
      persons with special needs 20
   Other special services 22

Baggage, carry-ons,
    bicycles, skis, etc. 24

A note about packing 25

Be alert for unmanned stations . . . 25

Animals on the train 26

Chapter 4
Trip Planning 29

Important points to remember
    when booking travel 30

Things to bring 33

Chapter 5
Getting the Best Fare 37

Ask the right questions 37

Types of Fares 38

Air/Rail travel 41

This family made its
    travel dollar go far 41

The USA Rail Pass 42

Chapter 6
Group Travel and
    Amtrak Reservations 47

Booking group travel 47

Train travel information
    at your finger tips 48

A little known way to
    book a sleeper 49

Chapter 7

Preparing to Board the Train 53
 Call before going to the station 53
 Before and after boarding 54
 Your coach ticket 55
 Luggage handling 55

Chapter 8

Eating on the Train 59
 Eating in the diner 59
 Food and drink in the lounge 61
 Eating at your coach seat 62
 Your Private Garden on the Train . . 63

Chapter 9

Keeping Fit and Comfortable
on the Train 65
 Stretching 65
 Sleeping on the train 66
 To smoke or not to smoke 68
 Traveler's stretches 69

Chapter 10

Entertainment on the Train 81

Chapter 11

Special Concerns of Train Travelers . . 83
 If you get lost on the train 83
 Ticket refunds and cancellations . . . 84
 Commendations and complaints . . . 85
 Lost and found 86
 Routine station stops 87

Your Chicago stopover 88

Chapter 12
Questions Passengers Often Ask . . . 91

Chapter 13
The Train Crew 99
   Operating crew 99
   On-board service crew 100

Chapter 14
Other Sources of
Passenger Train Information 103

Chapter 15
Tipping 105
   By way of history 105
   The practice today 106

Chapter 16
Passenger Trains in
America's Future? 109

Index 113

Order Form

Introduction

Considering a train trip in the USA? If you're not going on a commuter line, then you will be riding on Amtrak—the federally-owned and operated rail passenger service corporation. More and more people are "Amtraking" and finding it a wonderful way to travel. If you want to enjoy long distance train travel and experience minimum hassles, you will benefit from reading this book. In my fifth year as an Amtrak train attendant, I work about twelve days a month, traveling the western routes. Hands-on experience gives me an insiders's perspective on train travel.

While working on the train, I frequently meet passengers who are encountering difficulties that could be avoided if they had certain information. After advising passengers and answering the same questions trip after trip, I decided to write a guide to help people get the most from their time spent on the train - that is, to help them be more comfortable, get more for their travel dollar, save time, and, generally, to have an enjoyable trip.

Many passengers are unsure what to expect and what guidelines to observe upon boarding the train. They are not familiar with some of the unique benefits of "Amtraking", and how to take advantage of them. This book answers these and other important questions. It offers the reader a close-up view of Amtrak trains, with tips and suggestions to make them fun and affordable. Use it as a handy reference, especially before you go on your next long distance train trip.

Mauris L. Emeka, *drawing by:*
Justin L. Emeka

...Twas fun playing the harmonica for a few minutes this morning as we pulled off from Whitefish, Montana. As the train gained momentum, it produced a cadence that went well with my harmonica rendition of "When The Saints Go Marchin' In".

...Soon the train got up to speed, and the beat of the wheels was too fast to go with the song; but it was sure fun for a few moments.

...Along with the rhythmic sound of the wheels, I felt my body moving with the motion of the train, as my harmonica played this beautiful refrain.

The Author
On The Empire Builder
December 17, 1993

CHAPTER ONE / *The Magic of A Train*

I am often aware of the magic of a train—that smooth and relaxing feeling as it pulls off from the station, the bold look of the engine that goes and goes, and the smell of delicious hot cakes as you approach the dining car in the morning.

I like the rhythmic sound of the wheels, especially when it accents my harmonica playing. And in a society preoccupied with consumerism, high technology and impersonality, a train ride reminds me of when life was simpler. A train ride fosters a rare sense of community—a feeling that we're all in this together. It is a treat to experience the wide diversity in ages and cultural backgrounds of passengers and crew members. And while riding the rails, there is a great tendency to live in the present moment. That, too, is part of the magic of a train.

Still not convinced? Consider these other reasons to take the train on your next trip.

❑ Spacious reclining seats offer lots more leg room than airplanes or cars.

❑ Families and travel groups can have more fun together playing games, visiting the sight-seeing lounge and the diner, or taking in a movie after dinner.

❑ Trains provide a more relaxed atmosphere than airplanes or cars.

❑ The train is a fun and safe way for older children and teenagers to travel alone.

❑ The sight-seeing lounge, with it's expansive picture windows, provides an excellent way to see the countryside on most long distance trains. At times, it is like sitting at an ever-changing picture window. Some stretches of spectacular scenery cannot be reached by automobile. There are scenic canyons and river valleys between Denver and Salt Lake City that can only be seen from the train (or by hikers). The same is true of parts of Glacier National Park, Montana.

❑ Where else but on the train can you savor delicious meals while enjoying a changing panorama of interesting sights?

❑ Sleeper cars provide privacy and the extra amenities of a "hotel on wheels."

Meals are part of the sleeper car package. Deluxe rooms have a private toilet and shower; and on most trains, the economy rooms have access to a shower. Sleeper car passengers will especially enjoy being able to retire in a comfortable bed, falling asleep to the rhythmic sound of the train.

❑ The usual afternoon "hospitality hour" allows passengers to loosen up in the lounge.

❑ Long train trips provide a great opportunity for making new friends. That's another benefit of that shared community on a train.

*The Empire Builder takes the northern-most route from
Seattle to Chicago. Over some stretches near Cutbank,
Montana, one can look in the distance and see Canada.
Photo courtesy of National Railroad Passenger Association.*

CHAPTER TWO / *A Brief History of Passenger Trains*

The Early Years

Nearly one hundred years before the first automobile, there was rail travel. History books give different dates as to exactly when rail travel began, but it is certain that by 1825, this mode of transportation was a reality. It was in that year that Colonel John Stevens' steam-powered, wooden cogged wheel train carried passengers. Another early railroader, John B. Javis, made rail passenger travel faster and more comfortable. The Baltimore and Ohio offered the first American chartered passenger line in the early 1830s. Not long afterward, other eastern railroads pushed westward to the Mississippi River and beyond. These 'iron horses' truly transformed America.

In his book *Workin' On The Railroad*, Richard Reinhardt makes the point that from about 1829 to 1934, the railroad was without rival in occupying the center of public life in America. It was a key element in America's expansion from sea to sea. It helped transform deserts into farms, and farms into factories. The railroad closed the curtain on the last frontier in a way that was not possible by the horse drawn carriage which it replaced.

By the middle 1830s, the railroads linked principal cities such as Boston, Philadelphia, Chicago, Baltimore, and a large number of smaller cities east of the Mississippi. Trains made interstate commerce possible; they established and standardized our four time zones; and they transported raw materials, crops, and livestock in quantities and at speeds that had not been achieved before. Remember, this was more than one hundred years before those now familiar eighteen-wheelers that fill our freeways and the airplanes that leave contrails across our skies.

Until around 1850, passenger train travel was quite crude and uncomfortable. Open windows in the summer allowed engine smoke to enter the coaches, and wood stoves provided the only heat. Passenger trains were not equipped with restroom facilities, lounges or food cars, and not much thought was given to making overnight travel comfortable. The first sleeper cars, referred to as "bunk cars", were converted coaches that provided none of the convenience and amenities of sleeper cars that were later introduced. They did not have comfortable and neatly made beds, nor did they offer the services of a car attendant.

In 1858, a man named George M. Pullman entered the rail passenger travel business. He had traveled by train many times and was dissatisfied with the lack of passenger comforts. This led to the founding of the Pullman Sleeping Car Company. Designed and built with passenger comfort in mind, Pullman sleeping cars soon became the industry standard. The company stressed excellent service, passenger comfort, and safety. The reputation of the Pullman Company became virtually synonymous with quality and good value in rail travel. Passengers could now travel overnight and enjoy it.

1860 and After

A sleeping car named "The Pioneer" was one of the first made by Pullman. It revolutionized the industry with its superior construction, as well as it's polished wood interior, plush seats and carpeting. It was the first sleeping car to use linen. In contrast to cars made by other companies whose trucks had only four wheels and rubber shocks, the Pioneer was constructed with six-wheel trucks and strong springs for a more comfortable ride.

Beginning in the early 1860s, if you booked a sleeping car it was in a Pullman. The company offered services to its passengers that are remembered to this day by those who traveled by sleeper car in the early nineteen-hundreds. The Pullman Company specialized in sleeping cars only, but it had an effect on all the major railroad companies that offered passenger train services. Pullman motivated other railroad companies to offer more modern accommodations.

In their book *A Long Hard Journey*, Patricia and Fredrick McKissack mention three historic events that gave a boost to train travel. They were the Emancipation Proclamation of 1863, the death of President Abraham Lincoln in 1865, and the completion of the first intercontinental railroad in 1869.

Some four million persons of African ancestry were freed by the Emancipation Proclamation and many of these newly freed slaves and sons of former slaves flocked to George Pullman's new company. For roughly the first thirty-five years, Pullman paid no salary to these workers, who were glad for the opportunity to travel the country extensively and work for tips. They worked for tips only until around the turn of the century. Other railroad companies paid their African American workers minimally, about twenty percent of the wage rate paid to laborers nationally. By the early years of this century, the Pullman Company was reported to have been the largest single employer of African American labor. The company saved hundreds of thousands of dollars annually by not paying wages to porters and waiters in these early years. Needless to say, this helped establish the Pullman Company as a highly profitable business.

And what do former passengers have to say about the men who worked the Pullman sleepers and built a reputation that has lasted even to this day? I often ask older passengers to tell me what sticks in their minds about these men. Without exception, these workers were described as poised, gracious, gentle, obliging, eager to please. A lady in her seventies told me not long ago, "If Pullman porters had problems, they must have deposited them elsewhere before they came around us."

1862 was a good year in the growth of railroads. That was the year President Lincoln signed the Pacific Railroad Act, which made possible the completion of America's first intercontinental railroad. It made travel from coast to coast much faster. The final rails of the Union Pacific and Central Pacific Railroads were joined together in 1869 in Promontory, Utah. For the first time, this linked East with West, insuring that the railroads would be central to

America's westward expansion and industrial development. When President Lincoln was assassinated in 1865, the Pioneer sleeping car was part of the fallen President's funeral train that toured the country for weeks. This now famous funeral train proved to be invaluable advertisement for train travel, as hundreds of thousands of people along it's path got to see what travel by train could be like.

Another historic happening in railroad development occurred in 1869, when George Westinghouse received a patent for the air brake. The air brake, along with automatic switching and signal devices, made rail travel much safer, while enabling locomotives to pull heavier loads at faster speeds.

Motor Cars Replace Trains

Railroads were the dominant means of transportation during most of the first half of this century. In time, however, the introduction of private autos, trucks and airplanes had an increasingly negative impact on railroading. After World War II, passenger train travel tapered off considerably, and it continued to do so through the 1950s and 60s. By 1960, airline travel began to capture more of the travel market, and the advent of bank cards and airline travel cards made it possible for more people to "afford" this new means of travel. Also contributing to the decline of passenger rail travel was the fact that most railroad companies had decided, as early as the 1950s, that the big profits were to be made in freight and not in passenger operations.

So by 1965, the once bustling passenger train service that had helped usher in the industrial revolution and helped see the country through two world wars, had been reduced to a mere skeleton. The Pullman Company ceased passenger service operations in 1969.

Amtrak is Launched

By the late 1960s the United States Congress recognized that passenger train services had dwindled to almost nothing. They knew that this fast disappearing transportation system had served the national interest through two wars. (Hundreds of thousands of soldiers and sailors were transported by passenger train in the 1940s). So, in 1970, Congress passed legislation that created the National Railroad Passenger Corporation. The corporation adopted the name "Amtrak" as its trade name, and as of this writing the company operates scheduled trains in all states of the continental USA except Oklahoma, Maine, and South Dakota. This part public and part private corporation, with some 24,000 employees, continues to experience moderate growth as more people take to the rails.

Pictured here is a rail passenger car used in 1844. These cars were quite crude, they were constructed with very little suspension, and produced a rough ride. Reproduced from: "The Story of The Pullman Car," copyright 1917.

The Superliner II is Amtrak's latest addition to the fleet. About 190 of these new bi-level cars will be delivered and put into operation between 1994 and 1997. Photo courtesy of Bombardier Corp., Bensalem, PA.

CHAPTER THREE / *What's Available—Equipment and Services*

On a typical long haul train there are several types of cars, including coach, sleeper, diner, and lounge cars. On some trains one-half of the dining car is used as a diner and the other half for lounge services. Most train passengers buy simply a basic coach seat; others buy sleeper accommodations. All passengers enjoy the use of the diner and lounge facilities.

Coach Cars

The most common equipment on a passenger train is the coach car, called the chair car in the early days of railroading. This car has wide aisles, cushioned high back seats that recline and lots of leg room. There is considerably more space for each passenger than is available on the bus or airplane. A tray table is attached to the front of each seat; and there is a footrest, a leg rest, reading lights, and a call button for each seat.[1]

Restrooms are located downstairs in each car. For people with infants, there is a Baby Changer platform that drops from the wall in two of the bathrooms. Your car attendant will show you their exact location.

A water fountain is located beside the stairway, both up and downstairs. Trash receptacles are at both ends and in the middle of the car upstairs by the water fountain.

Located downstairs in certain cars is a special seating section where disabled persons and senior citizens may elect to sit. Of the several restrooms downstairs, one is large enough to accommodate a wheelchair, and it has a handrail for the convenience of mobility impaired passengers. If you wish to sit in the downstairs section, and are disabled or 62 years or older, be sure to let Amtrak reservations know this when you are booking your travel. No other common carrier goes to such lengths to meet the needs of passengers with physical impairments. Even a

---

[1] Throughout this book, when we refer to coach and sleeping car accommodations, we are talking about Amtrak's bi-level Superliner equipment. I am the most familiar with it, since I work on board this equipment, traveling the western routes.

Passengers enjoy the view from the upper level of the Superliner Sight Seeing Lounge car. The lower level (not shown) is also where passengers buy snacks, play cards, and visit.

portable wheelchair ramp is available to help wheelchair passengers on and off the train.

A luggage compartment is downstairs, just as you enter the car. There is also overhead luggage space, enough for a small to medium-sized suitcase, pillows, blankets and coats.

The car attendant will dim the overhead lights at around 10 P.M. to make it easier for passengers to sleep. He or she will also pass out pillows, for which there is no charge. If the temperature of the car is not to your liking, ask your attendant if adjustments can be made. Attendants can control the temperature within certain limits.

Occasionally, someone becomes sick on the train. The conductor and the chief of on-board

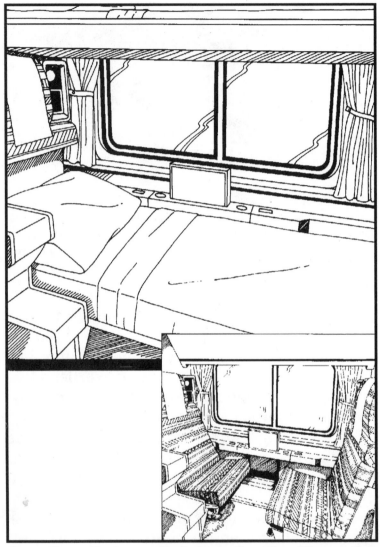

Superliner Economy Bedroom. Smaller illustration shows reclining seats for daytime travel. They make into the lower berth for night time sleeping, as shown in the larger illustration. There is also an upper berth. This room sleeps two persons.

services are immediately called if the matter is serious. They will make an announcement to ask any trained medical person on board to come forward. If the problem is serious enough, the conductor can radio ahead for mobile medics to meet the train.

It is the responsibility of the car attendant to keep the restrooms clean. If they are not clean and well stocked with paper products, any passenger should feel free to tactfully tell the attendant that such and such restroom needs attention. If there is still a problem with cleanliness of the restrooms, or with the tidiness of the car in general, passengers should speak with the chief of on-board services.

The toilet in each restroom is a mechanical device that is very sensitive. These toilets plug up if bulky items such as paper towels, sanitary napkins or cups are placed in them. Only human waste and tissue paper should be put in them. One clogged toilet can shut down the disposal system in the entire car.

Sleeper Car Accommodations

Passengers need to know from the outset that sleeper car fares include meals. When you buy sleeper accommodations, you in essence buy a room—a kind of hotel room on wheels. Say, for example, you buy an economy bedroom in the off-peak season (one-way) between Chicago and Denver for $129. The economy room actually sleeps two adults, each of whom must also pay the lowest one-way rail fare between Chicago and Denver. But the $129 room charge would be assessed only once. Again, both passengers, but not more than two, would be furnished meals in the diner during the trip.

Deluxe bedrooms, the family room, and the special bedroom for the physically impaired are also available. In addition, some eastern trains offer "slumber coaches" where your sleeping car seat makes down into a bed at night. "Slumber coaches" are the least expensive of sleeper car accommodations and the fare you pay does not include meals. Again, each passenger buys a coach ticket, but the room is paid for only once. The deluxe bedroom, which has its own bath and shower, provides sleeping and meals for three occupants. The family bedroom accommodates five persons and this includes meals as well. The special room sleeps two persons, and includes private bathroom, room for a wheelchair, and meals.[2]

---

[2] **NOTE**: For Additional information on sleeper car and coach services, see the publication *Discover The Magic: Amtrak's America*. Get a copy from your travel agent, or from Amtrak by calling Toll-free 1-800-USA RAIL, or 1-800-321-9887.

If you are booked in the sleeper, you'll be assisted by a car attendant for the duration of your trip. Your attendant is someone you can get to know quite well, because from the moment you step aboard until you arrive at your destination, this person will be of service to you. He or she will assist you in boarding the train, in securing your luggage, and will point out the location of your room.

The attendant will help maintain a comfortable room temperature, let out your bed at night, make it up in the morning, give you a wake up call if you desire, and make coffee and juice available in the morning. This person can also bring meals to your room when time permits. Highest priority for meal service in their rooms is the physically impaired and the elderly.

Each sleeper occupant is given a meal voucher shortly after boarding, and one room occupant must sign the voucher and present it to the dining car steward whenever going to the diner to eat. Once the voucher is signed, any of the room's occupants can present it to the dining car steward at mealtime. And, remember, whenever entering the dining car be sure to wait to be seated by a dining car crew member.

Dining Car and Lounge Car

All long haul trains have dining cars. Other trains that provide local service,say, from New York to Washington, DC., or from Chicago to St. Louis are equipped with a lounge car only. The dining car serves full service, sit down meals three times daily. The lounge car (often called the sight seeing lounge) offers sandwiches, soft drinks, alcoholic beverages and various snack items. Hours of service in the lounge car are from roughly 6:30 A.M. until about 11:30 P.M. On long haul trains, the dining car and lounge car are always situated next to each other and are near the center of the train.

Services for Senior Citizens and Those With Special Needs

Amtrak, more than any other common carrier, makes a special effort to offer travel that's affordable and practical for passengers 62 and over. The same is true for passengers who are in some way mobility-impaired.

Senior citizens and other passengers who require special assistance are sometimes concerned about climbing the stairs in Superliner cars; they are also concerned about boarding and detraining safely. This need not be a problem, because the train attendant is available to assist. Also, in Superliner cars, as well as in single-level coach and sleeper cars, there is a restroom large enough to accommodate a wheelchair. These restrooms are equipped with hand railing and call button, and are located close to the special assistance seating section in superliner cars.

Superliner sleeper cars are equipped with a special bedroom to accommodate a disabled person and one other passenger. This room has its own toilet, and is laid out for the convenience of someone who needs special assistance. The attendant can bring meals and assist in other ways, but if passengers are very ill or otherwise require fairly continuous assistance, then they must be accompanied by someone who can assist them at all times.

Most coach and sleeper cars are equipped with a portable wheelchair ramp for wheelchair passengers. In the larger stations, redcap porters help wheelchair-bound passengers from the station to the train. In the smaller stations, one of the station keepers will often assist and, as always, the car attendant will help passengers onto and off of the train.

Train attendants have a number of responsibilities that keep them quite busy. But for passengers who are disabled, ill or elderly, they will make every effort to provide them food service and other assistance as needed. Again, if a passenger requires continuous assistance,

however, he or she will need to travel with
someone who can provide it. Amtrak offers fare
discounts to senior citizens , as well as to persons who are mobility impaired. Read more
about this in chapter five.

Other Special Services

As was already mentioned, the restrooms
are located downstairs by the special seating
section. Therefore, passengers traveling in the
downstairs section do not have to climb stairs
to get to the bathroom. Passengers may bring
self-contained oxygen equipment, but this
equipment may not be dependent on train-gen-
erated power.

For persons who are hearing-impaired,
Amtrak provides a telephone reservations and
information number for teletypewriters. This
service is offered twenty-four hours a day,
seven days a week. The toll-free T.D.D. number
is 1-800-523-6590. In Pennsylvania, the number is 1-800-562-6960.

Passengers requiring special meals involving low sodium, diabetic or kosher preparations
can request these meals when they book their
travel. It is best to make special meal requests
at least three or four days before departure;
and since special meal requests are infrequent,
you should ask the reservations clerk to high-
light this request in the computer when making

your reservations. This will call it to the attention of commissary and dining car personnel, so the proper food will be brought on board.

Additional Benefits of the Special Seating Section

Senior citizens, as well as middle-aged passengers, are fond of train travel, since it often reminds them of train trips they took in earlier years. The downstairs special seating section in the Superliner offers space for thirteen passengers. On a long trip, the passengers seated in this section get to know one another quite well; they often develop friendships, exchange experiences, and have sing-alongs. As a train attendant, I enjoy returning to this special seating section often during the day, sometimes sitting for a time, playing my harmonica. Some passengers will sing-along as I play tunes like "The Tennessee Waltz", or "America The Beautiful." Others just listen as they enjoy the ride.

Just before passengers arrive at their respective destinations, they sometimes exchange addresses before bidding each other a warm farewell. Train travel is rather unique that way.

Baggage, Carry-Ons, Bicycles, Skis, Etc.

You can check your baggage on the train. Each ticketed passenger is entitled to check, free-of-charge, up to three pieces of baggage. The bags are not to exceed 75 pounds each or 150 pounds total weight.

For a $5.00 handling charge, passengers may take a bicycle in lieu of a piece of baggage. Bicycle boxes are available by Amtrak at no additional charge to the passenger. If you have skis, a musical instrument, or a baby carrier, there's no problem bringing such items along on the train. There is room in the overhead luggage racks on each coach car for one or two medium-sized suitcases per passenger. In addition, there is room in the luggage racks downstairs in Superliner coaches.

If you have a berth in the sleeper car, you will want to leave most of your carry-on baggage in the luggage rack downstairs by the vestibule. Except in the special room and the deluxe rooms, there is not a lot of space to accommodate more than a small piece of luggage in the sleeper berths.

When you check your bags, you will be given a claim check with a three-letter symbol indicating the city to where your bags have been checked. For example, CHI is Chicago, PDX is Portland, NOL is New Orleans. Make sure the three-letter symbol on the claim check designates the city where you want your bags to go. Say, for instance, you're going to Klamath Falls, Oregon. Then make sure you are not handed a claim check that designates Kansas City. Also, be sure to safeguard your baggage claim check(s), as you will need one claim check to reclaim each checked bag at the end of your trip. At most stations, your checked bags will be brought to you at the luggage claim area about five to twenty minutes after you arrive at your destination.

A Note About Packing

When packing, be sure to include items such as medicines, toiletries, and other personal things in your carry-on bags, not in the bags to be checked. If, however, you have an extremely urgent need to retrieve something from a piece of your checked baggage, then see your attendant and/or the conductor. If the matter is sufficiently urgent, it may be possible to accommodate your request.

Be Alert for Unmanned Stations

There are a few unmanned stops along most Amtrak routes. In other words, there is no station keeper on duty to sell tickets or to handle baggage. You cannot check bags to these stops. Unmanned stops are designated in the system timetable and they are also noted in the Amtrak reservations computer. If your final station stop happens to be at an unmanned location, then you should not try to check your bags but plan to carry them on the train with you.

Not long ago, a young man on my coach car got off the train at The Dalles, Oregon. Unfortunately, his luggage was checked to Portland, Oregon. When this young man boarded the train back in the Midwest, he was told that the town of The Dalles was an unmanned station and that he could not check his luggage to that stop. So, it was decided to check it to Portland since that was the next manned station stop. Little did this passenger realize, however, that The Dalles is not a suburb of Portland but is 86 miles away. To avoid this kind of inconvenience, be sure to carry your luggage on board whenever you are getting off at a station that is unstaffed.

Animals on the Train

Seeing eye dogs and hearing ear dogs are the only animals permitted to be brought on the train. When someone brings one of these dogs on board, passengers are urged not to bother these dogs, or feed or pet them. These are actually "working dogs" and, in most cases, their masters prefer that animal lovers not interfere with these devoted helpers.

Superliner Deluxe Bedroom. Smaller illustration shows reclining seats for daytime travel. They make into the lower berth for night time sleeping, as shown in the larger illustration. There is also an upper berth. This room sleeps three persons

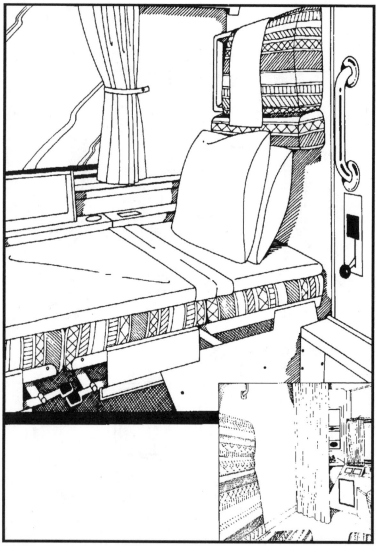

Superliner Special Bedroom (Equipped for mobility-impaired passengers). Seats recline like the Economy Room to make into lower berth. It also contains an upper berth along with sink and toilet. Sleeps two persons, and is considerably more spacious than the Economy Room.

CHAPTER FOUR / *Trip Planning*

A friend once told me that when she first considered taking a train trip, she talked with a neighbor who had recently traveled by rail. After that she called her travel agency, and from these two conversations she got an idea of what to expect. Once she actually got on the train and started on her way, my friend said she was very glad she had done a bit of pre-planning. This chapter is designed to assist a person in planning a trip by train.

You, too, can get the ball rolling toward your next trip by talking with someone you know who recently traveled by train. And if you contact a travel agent, be sure to chose one familiar with booking train travel. Since travel agents book mainly airlines and cruise ships, many of them are not familiar with the ins and outs of train travel. Some travel agents are reasonably familiar with the rules of train travel, yet have never actually traveled by train themselves. So find out when your travel agent last took a trip by train. And if you are speaking with an Amtrak reservations clerk, ask him or her the same question.

Suppose you are planning an extensive trip involving the train, a hotel stay, and perhaps a car rental. You may want to call Amtrak's Great American Vacations at 1-800-321-9887. They will tailor a rail package based on your specific travel desires. When you call, be sure to have in mind your travel dates, any stopover locations, and the length of time you wish to stay at various locations. Also, don't hesitate to request a copy of the booklet, *Amtrak's America*. It shows photos of trains (inside and outside) and provides extensive train travel tips. Request your free copy by writing to: Amtrak's America, Distribution Center (Dept. 43), Itaska, IL 60143.

Important Points to Remember When Booking Your Travel

❑ It is very important to book sleeping car accommodations early. On many western routes Amtrak does not have enough sleeping car berths to meet the demand, so try to make your plans as early as three to six months in advance.

❑ Reconfirm your sleeper car room before going to the station. I recommend that you reconfirm your room by calling Amtrak reservations (1-800-USA-RAIL) approximately twenty-four hours before the scheduled departure. Sometimes agents that handwrite Amtrak tickets fail to call Amtrak and tell them to reserve in the computer the particular room for which they've sold a ticket. If you are holding such a ticket, you might arrive at the train to find that some other passenger has also been ticketed for the same sleeper room. There was just such a mixup on a trip I worked. And though the matter was satisfactorily resolved, the problem could have been avoided if the passenger had called the reservations office to re-confirm his travel plans a few hours before leaving for the train station. The other lesson here is that if a travel agent *handwrites* your ticket for a sleeping berth, be sure he or she calls Amtrak reservations to put your room reservation in the computer.

❏ On-board service workers need to know in advance about passengers requiring special assistance. Passengers with wheelchairs, those on salt-free diets, and children traveling alone should make their needs known when booking reservations. If a passenger has health related needs, be sure to specify lower level seating on all Superliner trains. Your agent will note this with your ticketing information in the reservations computer.

❑ If your travel itinerary includes making connections from one train to another, make sure you allow sixty minutes or more between connecting trains, because Amtrak will then guarantee your connection. That means if you miss your connecting train because of the late arrival of your incoming train, Amtrak will take responsibility for arranging alternative travel plans to your destination. In some instances, this involves providing hotel lodging for misconnecting passengers who must catch their connecting train the next day.

Amtrak has some of the best and most experienced operating crews to be found anywhere, but there are a number of things that can make trains late. And, quite often, a train's tardiness has nothing to do with the efficiency of the train crew or the reliability of the equipment. I usually recommend that passengers allow a minimum of two or three hours connecting time between trains. This is recommended especially for passengers arriving on long haul trains from distant cities such as New York, New Orleans and Los Angeles, and who then connect through Chicago for other points. Ask your Amtrak ticket agent to attempt to find out the actual arrival time record of your in-bound train over the last five or ten days. A knowledgeable and candid agent or reservations clerk can sometimes shed light on such a question.

Things To Bring

When you take an extended train trip, one that lasts more than about six hours, there are certain things you will want to consider bringing along.

❖ A Blanket—This is the one item you don't want to be without if you're going to be on the train overnight. Regulating the heat and air conditioning in coach cars late at night is sometimes a problem.

❖ A Neck Pillow—Also, very helpful for enhancing your comfort by preventing stiff neck. A picture of this item is shown here. Neck pillows can be found in the luggage section of many department stores, or sometimes in drugstores. Or, you can order one by

This Neck Pillow Enhances Travel Comfort

filling out the order form in the back of this book.

❖ If you plan to take pictures, be sure to bring along enough film. There are very few stops along the way where you can buy any.

❖ For entertainment, bring cards, drawing sets, hand puppets for small children, books, letter writing stationary and stamps, and other pursuits that interest you.

❖ Bring along fresh fruits. As well as being tasty, they help your body maintain proper hydration in the dry air-conditioned environment of the train.

❖ A change of clothes and carry-along toiletries will help you feel fresher on a long trip.

Finally, here's an idea that serves me well on every train trip. Plan your trip well, but don't try to control every aspect of it. Regardless of how extensive you plan, it's really the way you spontaneously interact with fellow passengers and crew members that determines how much enjoyment you will get. So get adequate rest the night before departing, assume an upbeat attitude, and you'll most likely have a fun experience.

The ICE Train allowed Amtrak passengers to test gourmet dining and at-seat video features.

Courtesy of National Railroad Passenger Corp.

Amtrak completed an extremely successful revenue test this past year of a Swedish X2000 tilting high-speed trainset and a German ICE (Inter City Express) high-speed trainset. Both operated in revenue service at 135 mph, 10 mph above the limit for existing *Metroliners*. Extensive customer surveying was performed and will be reflected in the specifications Amtrak will soon complete for the new trainsets.

Because Amtrak is subject to Buy America provisions and strict United States safety standards, Amtrak cannot acquire off-the-shelf European high-speed rail equipment. As a result, Amtrak's procurement will generate an entirely new, built-in-America generation of high-speed rail equipment that is likely to set the standard for all high-speed rail equipment

CHAPTER FIVE / *Getting the Best Fare*

Ask the Right Questions

The train can be an economical way to travel. You need not be a travel expert to get the best fare, but you do need to be aware of the commonly offered fares. A few key questions will let your agent know you are serious about getting the most for your travel dollar.

✓ What discount fares might I qualify for?

✓ What are the restrictions that apply to this or that fare?

✓ Are there any promotional specials currently in effect?

✓ Am I approaching the off-peak reduced fares season?

Say, for instance, you want to travel from New York City to Albuquerque, New Mexico. When you contact a ticket agent, let him or her know that you're looking to purchase the best discounted one-way or roundtrip ticket. When the agent quotes a fare, ask what type it is. Let the agent (or reservations clerk) know if you can be somewhat flexible about your departure date, especially if it can produce a savings in your ticket price. Be sure to mention if you happen to be a senior citizen, an adult traveling with children, in the military, or mobility-impaired. Ask if there is more than one route for getting from New York City to Albuquerque, and which route gets you there fastest with the fewest connections. By offering pertinent information and asking the right questions, you are helping your agent help you.

Recently, a woman on a train on which I was working traveled from Chicago to Seattle. About an hour before her 2,500-mile trip ended, I happened to mention to my passenger that she could have taken a different train from Chicago and gotten to Seattle about eight hours earlier. She seemed amazed and her first reply was "Why didn't they tell me that?." Asking the right questions of your ticket agent can be beneficial.

Types of Fares

Here are some common types of train fares.

❑ Regular Adult Fare

❑ Excursion

❏ All Aboard America
❏ Special All Aboard America
❏ Promotional
❏ Military
❏ Disabled
❏ Senior Citizen
❏ Child's Fare

The Regular Adult fare, the most common, and most expensive is the fare that your ticket agent will generally quote you when you ask how much it costs to travel from point A to point B. All the other fares are discounted down from the Regular Adult fare. There is usually a limited number of seats allocated on each train to be sold at discount fares, and they often carry restrictions such as no refund if they are not used, or no opportunity to change travel plans later. Be sure your agent or reservations clerk explains this to you, so as to avoid surprises later. And when looking for a travel bargain, the earlier a person starts shopping the better.

Consider on-peak and off-peak travel. You can choose to travel during off-peak times and save from twenty to thirty percent off the regular fare. Exact dates of on-peak and off-peak seasons vary somewhat from year to year, but on-peak is roughly June through the second week of August, and again from about December the through the first week of January. Off-peak fares are in effect all other times of the year.

If you are a senior citizen, age 62 or older, you can receive an additional senior citizen's discount (15 percent as of this writing) on top of any discounted fare you may already have received. For example, a promotional fare may qualify you for a reduced rate ticket from New Orleans to Chicago; but the senior citizen's discount entitles you to an additional 15 percent discount off the promotional fare. Senior citizen's train tickets are undoubtedly among the best travel values to be found.

Disabled persons and military personnel are entitled to twenty-five percent discount off the regular fare. If you are planning roundtrip travel, however, it may be more economical to purchase the All Aboard America fare or possibly an excursion fare. Your ticket agent can look up the various fares that apply and suggest the most economical one.

Always ask about the All Aboard America fare. This very popular discounted fare lets you make three stopovers, and your travel must be completed in forty-five days. The price for the All Aboard America ticket depends on what zones you travel in, and whether you are traveling in on-peak or off-peak season. The All Aboard America fare consistently represents one of the best travel deals offered by Amtrak.

At the end of this chapter is a map showing the three zones associated with this type of fare.

Also, be sure to inquire if there is an excursion fare, promotional fare, or the Special All Aboard America fare. These fares allow considerable savings when you can get them. If you are traveling as a family, children up to the age of 15 (who are traveling with adults) go for half the fare of whatever the adult paid. Therefore, a family can realize much better savings here than with other types of common carriers.

Air/Rail Travel

Some travelers like the idea of taking the train in one direction, and the plane in the other direction. If so, they can ask the ticket agent about the new Air/Rail combination travel package, great for those who want to see the countryside but have limited time. This would allow you to go by train and return by airplane (or visa versa).

This Family Made Its Travel Dollar Go Far

You can get a lot of value from a travel dollar when you are aware of what is possible in terms of rail fares and various services. I rode with a family of four who traveled on an All Aboard America fare between Chicago and the west coast during off-peak season. They also purchased one economy room, entitling two persons to meals as well as sleeping berths. They alternated their sleeping times in the economy room. So, by purchasing a single economy room, this family enjoyed a good deal of sleeping car comfort with some complimentary meals.

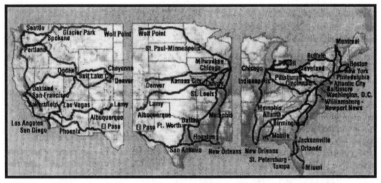

Shown here is a breakdown of the three zones that apply to the All Aboard America fare.

USA Rail Pass

For persons living in countries other than the United States or Canada, and who wish to experience America's vastness and natural beauty, there is no better travel value than the Amtrak Rail Pass. You must have a valid passport issued outside the United States or Canada to purchase this pass.

As of this writing, you could purchase a 30-day nationwide rail pass with unlimited stopovers for $319, or a 15-day rail pass for $218. It is possible to buy a pass covering only the western states or only the eastern states for roughly $100 less than the fares just mentioned. The price of the rail pass is also affected by on-peak and off-peak seasons, so check with an agent for the particulars.

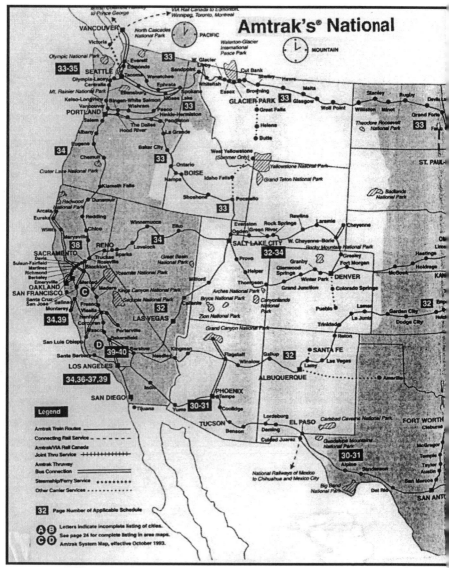

This is a broad outline of Amtrak's Rail Passenger
and towns served. A much more detailed map is found

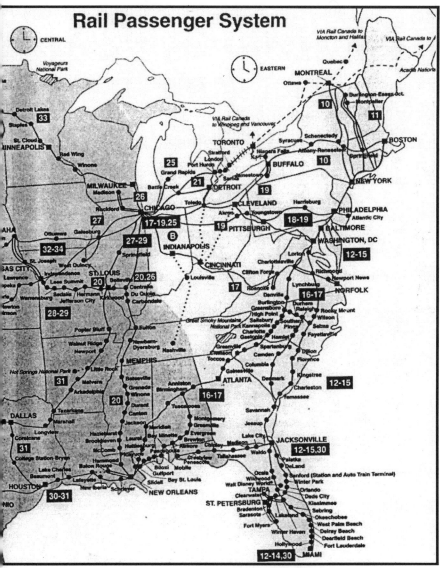

System. It does not include a complete listing of cities in the current copy of Amtrak's National Timetable.

Many of Amtrak's first trains, such as the Broadway Limited departing Chicago, resembled rainbows, due to the diverse paint schemes of the railroads that owned them before.

Courtesy of National Railroad Passenger Corp.

CHAPTER SIX / *Group Travel and Amtrak Reservations*

Booking Group Travel

If you are traveling with fifteen or more persons, consider Amtrak's group travel option. The first fifteen members of the group receive the best fare available, and the sixteenth member (usually the group leader) travels free. Groups are pre-boarded and seated in the same car together, and they can get a ten percent discount off dining car meals when they order and pre-pay for their meals with their group ticket purchase. Amtrak accommodates a number of ski groups, bike touring groups, and convention goers. If you have enough travelers, find out the details by calling 1-800-USA-1GRP. The line is open from 8:30 A.M. to 5:00 P.M. eastern time.

When you buy a group ticket, be sure the agent lets the Amtrak reservations computer know that a group is involved. If your ticket agent fails to enter a "group code" in the computer, your group will probably not be seated together. Make sure the ticket agent enters the number in the group and the name of the group leader. Also, have your ticket agent note in the computer any special services that might be needed—such as senior citizens requiring assistance, or ski groups with equipment, for example. This way, when train crew members read the loading manifest, they will know to reserve a block of seats together and to anticipate special needs such as extra storage space.

Train Travel Information At Your Finger Tips

If your travel agent is connected with the Amtrak reservations computer, then be sure to ask him or her to access any pertinent information that might be helpful to you. For example, the Amtrak reservations computer stores information about local transportation and points of interest in various cities. The agent accesses it by calling up the "profile screen" for the city you are interested in.

If you're traveling to Chicago, for example, you can find out from the city "profile screen" that Chicago's O'Hare Airport can be reached via the O'Hare Rapid Transit train. For $1.25 passengers can board the train at Clinton and Congress streets, just two blocks south of Chicago's Union Station, and arrive at O'Hare Airport in thirty-five to forty minutes. "City profile" information in Amtrak's reservations computer may call your attention to the world famous Sears Tower, just two blocks from Union Station.

A Little-Known Way to Book Sleeper Accommodations when the Computer Shows 'None Available'

Since sleeper car rooms are usually in high demand, it is often difficult to get them unless you reserve months in advance. Being creative, however, it is sometimes possible to book a berth in the sleeper even when the computer says none is available.

Suppose, for example, you want an economy room from Seattle to Los Angeles. The agent queries the reservations computer and learns that none is available for the day requested. You might then ask the agent to try to secure sleeper reservations for part of the way. By looking at the schedule for the Coast Starlight, the train that services Seattle to LA, you note that it leaves Seattle at 10:40 A.M. and arrives in LA the next evening at 7:40 P.M. Your next step is to ask the agent to query the computer to see if a room is available between various scheduled stops between Seattle and LA. Ask especially about room availability between two smaller towns that are fairly close to Seattle and to LA.

After checking the Coast Starlight schedule again, you would ask the agent to check the computer for a room between, say, Albany, Oregon and Salinas, California; or between, say, Vancouver, Washington and San Louis Obispo, California; or perhaps between Chemult, Oregon and Santa Barbara, California; or even between Salem, Oregon and San Jose, California. It's possible that the computer will show room availability between two towns in one of these four sets. If you get a room between either of these two intermediate towns, its true that you would not have the benefit of it all the way from Seattle to LA. But you would at least enjoy comfortable sleeping accommodations for the one night you're on the train.

If you are successful in getting get a room from, say, Salem, Oregon to Salinas, California, then it simply means you'll ride from Seattle to Salem and from Salinas to LA in coach accommodations. The rest of your trip will be in your sleeping berth. In short, you would enjoy a room (which includes meals in the diner) during most of your trip.

It pays to keep an open mind to various possibilities when you're looking for sleeper accommodations. When you query the computer about rooms between small station stops near where your trip begins and ends, it sometimes reveals space it did not show before. But the computer cannot give you that space unless you ask your agent to ask the computer if the space is available.

This building formerly served as the train station at Green River, Wyoming, a town of only 12,000 population. Like many other deactivated train stations all across America, this distinctive structure stands as a reminder of yesteryear's bustling passenger train business.

This station serves Salem, Oregon. Built in 1916, it is located a few blocks from the Oregon State Capital Building.

CHAPTER SEVEN /

Preparing To Board The Train

Call Before Going To The Station

If friends or relatives are picking you up at your destination point, you should advise them to call toll-free 1-800-USA-RAIL to reconfirm the train arrival time. In the event your arriving train is going to be late, the party picking you up would probably appreciate knowing in advance.

Similarly, if you are taking the train and have a long distance to drive to get to the station, you should also call the toll-free number. They can tell you if your departing train is going to leave on time. And please note: It is very important you arrive at the station at least one-half hour before your train is supposed to depart.

Before and After
Boarding The Train

The Historic King Street Station in Seattle, Washington. Photo by Gabriel Emeka.

Before boarding the train you will be told either the track number or location of your train. Always identify your train by number and name. Occasionally, there are two trains going to the same city. For example, the Southwest Chief and the Desert Wind both depart Chicago for Los Angeles in the afternoon. They take vastly different routes and one arrives in Los Angeles six hours before the other. So in this case, travelers going to Los Angeles need to know their correct train name and number.

When you first board the train (whether in coach or sleeper) it is important that you remain in your seat until the conductor comes around and picks up your ticket. This usually takes no more than ten to fifteen minutes, after which time you are free to move about the train.

Your Coach Ticket

When you buy a regular coach ticket it will have the words "reserve coach" printed on it. This ticket simply entitles you to a coach seat, although no specific seat is reserved for you. You may board the train and claim any coach seat that has not already been claimed. You can tell if a seat has already been claimed by the presence of a "seat check" just above it. You will recognize it as a colored rectangular card with a 3-letter city code printed on it. There will usually be the number 1 or 2 on the "seat check", indicating that one or two seats have already been claimed at that location.

Luggage Handling

Suppose you have arrived in Chicago, the hub of the Amtrak system, and are connecting to another train going south or east; and let's assume your bags were checked through to your final destination. You need not bother to reclaim them in Chicago, since your checked bags will automatically be transferred to the appropriate train.

If your train arrives at its connecting point late, your bags will be put on the next available

*Luggage about to be loaded onto the train at Seattle's
King Street Station. Photo by Gabriel Emeka.*

train going to your destination. In that case you
would most likely receive your checked bags
the day after you arrive at your final destination.

To help insure that checked bags are at
their final destination when the traveler arrives, some passengers check their bags
twenty-four hours before they depart. It is usually not necessary to do this. But it is not a bad
idea, especially if you're not too far from the
train station from which you are departing, and
if your connecting time is critical.

Amtrak station Serving Olympia-Lacey, Washington. This newly constructed award-winning station was built largely with local contributions and donated labor. Photo courtesy of Washington State Dept. of Transportation (Rail Branch).

(Below) San Diegan trains hug the Pacific Coast offering travelers spectacular views.

CHAPTER EIGHT /*Eating On The Train*

Eating In The Diner

There is a full service dining car on all long distance trains, and eating there can be an enjoyable experience. You can enjoy tasty dishes often while taking in beautiful scenery. Imagine dining on board the Empire Builder as it leaves Seattle bound for Chicago. While traveling along the picturesque Puget Sound waterway, you can enjoy an evening meal while watching the sun retire behind the Olympic Mountains. Enjoy breakfast the next morning as you travel through Glacier National Park in northwestern Montana.

To check if a particular train has a dining car, ask the person who is booking your reservations, or look at the train's schedule, at the bottom is a section that describes the services provided.

When entering the diner, be sure to wait to be seated by a member of the dining car staff, usually a lively and outgoing lot. Also, be aware that the dining car frequently fills to capacity, especially during the first seating of most meals. Be prepared to meet and talk with fellow passengers as you dine. After you are seated, the dining car steward will give you a meal check that shows all the meal selections and their prices. On some trains you will be instructed to circle your meal selection in ink and on other trains you must tell the waiter your selections and he or she will circle the selection for you. Only full course meals are served in the diner, and there is no a la carte service. For lighter fare such as soup, and sandwiches you will need to go to the lounge car.

Meals on some long distance trains are served using china, glassware, and linen. As of this writing, the trains that include these accommodations in their dining cars are the Auto Train, Lakeshore Limited (New York City section), Broadway Limited, Capital Limited, Crescent, Coast Starlight, Empire Builder, Zephyr, Southwest Chief, and Sunset Limited.

Breakfast is served on most trains from approximately 6:30 to 9:30 A.M. and it costs around $4 to $6. It is not until around 8 A.M. that a PA announcement is made indicating the dining car is open, although breakfast actually starts much earlier. Lunch is from noon until around 1:30 P.M., and the cost is from roughly $5 to $7. Dinner, which is by reservation only, is usually served from 5:30 until 7:30 P.M. and later. It costs approximately $9 to $14, depending on your selection.

It is easy to overeat at dinner time, as servings are often generous. Some travelers may want to remember this, especially if they tend to have trouble sleeping on the train.

Amtrak can accommodate special meal requests. If you desire a vegetarian entree there is usually one non-meat selection on the lunch and dinner menus. Should you desire low cholesterol breakfast you may order oatmeal, toast and juice, or a fruit dish. If you require, for instance, a lowfat meal or a kosher meal be sure to request it forty-eight to seventy-two hours before your train leaves. When you arrive at the station to board the train it is a good idea to re-confirm your special meal request with the ticket agent.

Food and Drink in the Lounge Car

All long distance trains have a lounge car or a combination diner/lounge car. If you desire something less than a full course meal, the lounge is where will find it. You can buy sandwiches, soft drinks, and many snack items. The lounge (or club car as some call it) also sells alcoholic beverages. Passengers typically go to the lounge to eat, drink, socialize, and view the scenery. Incidentally, passengers are not permitted to consume their own alcoholic beverages that they brought aboard, except in the privacy of their sleeping accommodations.

Eating At Your Coach Seat

If you are in sleeper accommodations all meals are included in the price of your ticket, and you will be given a meal voucher to present to the steward when you go for each meal. Coach passengers may find it practical to bring some of their own food. However, this must be consumed at their seats. Those who like fresh fruit should bring it with them as there is very little for sale on the train. Also, do not expect Amtrak to either heat or refrigerate your private food. It is possible, however, to obtain limited quantities of ice. If you need ice, check with your car attendant or go to the lounge.

Riding on the train, though less confining than other forms of travel, is still a sedentary activity, and there is the tendency to overeat during prolonged inactivity. Based on personal experience, I caution you against 'passing the time away' eating and snacking excessively, since it may cause you to arrive at your destination feeling sluggish.

Your Private Garden On The Train?

Sometimes—about four days before leaving home on a train trip—I put lentil, mung beans, or alfalfa seeds in a pint jar to sprout. By the day I'm ready to hit the rails, I have sprouting plants to take along in the same jar. They continue to sprout and grow with daily rinsing with water. I eat these plants starting the first or second day, often sharing them, as others seem surprised that someone brought along their own "private garden."

Long distance train rides can rob the body of vital nutrients. Fresh foods that are easily digested help restore them.

Courtesy of National
Railroad Passenger Corp.

*New Superliner II cars which
began to roll off the assembly line
this year will help improve the
quality of Amtrak service.*

CHAPTER NINE / *Keeping Fit and Comfortable On The Train*

Stretching Routines

As a train attendant who travels about 11,000 miles per month over Amtrak's western routes, I know the importance of keeping fit and comfortable while on board. When you are a passenger for more than a day, there is a chance of experiencing stiffness after an overnight ride. Walking to and from the dining car and lounge car helps one stay limber, but stretching also helps alleviate stiffness. At the end of this chapter is a series of "traveler's stretches" that the reader will surely find useful.

These stretches can be done on the train at your seat, while standing by the train when you get out for a rest stop, and in the privacy of your sleeping accommodations. One should refrain from doing stretching, however, when the train is traveling over rough and bumpy tracks. Excessive bouncing motion will cause the muscles being stretched to contract and stiffen. When done properly, stretching facilitates blood circulation in the legs, neck and shoulders. It is therefore very beneficial when a person is traveling long distances.

Sleeping On The Train

There is something very satisfying and even magical about crawling into a freshly made bed in the sleeper car and having the familiar rhythm and sounds of the train carry you off to sleep. There's nothing quite like the feeling of being able to retire in comfort while the train pushes on through the night. When lying in bed, you are more conscious of the engine sound and the engineer's whistle way up ahead. If you are traveling over smooth track, you may fall asleep in a matter of seconds.

What is it like to start your day on the train after a reasonably restful night? It can be an experience that humbles you, and makes you aware of the beauty and vastness of this land. Consider waking up to a truly magnificent sunrise as Amtrak's California Zephyr takes you westward across America's vast heartland in time to arrive in Denver for breakfast. And, as you look toward the front of the train, the Rocky Mountains gradually come into view, offering a majestic sight to remember. Or, imagine waking up to the sight of mountains, streams, and wildlife near Glacier National Park, Montana.

Sleeping in the coach car is less comfortable. You may not be able to stretch out into the seat beside you because someone may be occupying it. Occasionally, the temperature may be a bit cool, especially as the night grows old. Let's face it, sleeping in the coach car will probably not be the most enjoyable part of the train ride. In spite of that, there are things you can do to make the experience somewhat less of a hassle.

First, be sure to take a blanket. Otherwise, you can purchase one on the train for approximately $8. Some passengers stay warm at night by bringing a light sleeping bag instead of a blanket. In addition, you may want to bring your own pillow. Your coach attendant gives a pillow to each passenger, but it is small, so some passengers bring their own pillow. I also recommend a neck pillow which provides considerable comfort to the neck, since you are sitting upright for an extended time. My wife will absolutely not go on a train trip without her neck pillow!

If you are not detraining during the night, you may feel free to spend the evening in the lounge car. It sometimes offers a more comfortable alternative for sleeping once most of the passengers have returned to their respective cars.

The suggestions mentioned here will surely enhance your comfort while on the train. Plan ahead, and keep them in mind for your next trip.

To Smoke Or Not To Smoke

The issue of smoking is surely a problem for all common carriers, and passenger trains are no exception. On the one hand, common carriers want to welcome all passengers without alienating those who smoke. At the same time, there is increasing social pressure against smoking. In the spring of 1993, Amtrak started banning smoking on routes that were 4-1/2 hours or less in duration. Smoking policy on long distance trains has changed several times in recent years, all in an attempt to strike a balance in considering those who smoke and those who do not.

You may smoke cigarettes in the privacy of your sleeping car accommodations or in designated areas in either the lounge car or certain coach cars. When smoking in their sleeping car rooms, passengers are asked to close their doors, in consideration for passengers in nearby rooms who do not smoke. In general, smoking is permitted in specially designated areas on the train, and that's most likely to be in the lounge car.

Traveler's Stretches

There are some important points to re-member about doing stretching routines. Do not stretch until it hurts, because this causes the muscles to stiffen, thus defeating your pur-pose. If you feel pain in the area that you're stretching, back-off. Make sure your muscles feel comfortable and relaxed at the time you are stretching. Try not to bounce or bob the muscles up and down while they are being stretched.

Start with head in a comfortable, aligned position. Slowly tilt head to left side to stretch muscles on side of neck. Hold stretch for 20-30 seconds. Feel a good, even stretch. Do not overstretch. Then tilt head to right side and stretch. Do two or three times to each side.

Interlace your fingers behind your head just above ear level. Gently use your hands and arms to pull your head forward to stretch the back of the neck. Hold for 3-5 seconds. Repeat 3-5 times. Hold only tensions that feel good. Do not stretch to the point of pain.

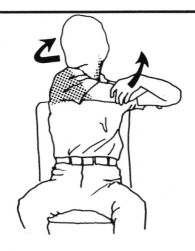

Hold your right arm just above the elbow with the left hand. Now gently pull elbow toward opposite shoulder as you look over your right shoulder. Hold stretch for 10 seconds. Do both sides.

To stretch the back of your neck move your chin into your chest. Hold position for 20-30 seconds while being relaxed. Do not use force. Feel good tensions of stretch. Repeat twice.

From a well-aligned position, feel an easy stretch in the front of your neck by lifting your chin upward, as you tilt the back of your head downward. Hold only tensions that feel good. Hold for 15 seconds, then return to starting aligned position. Do twice.

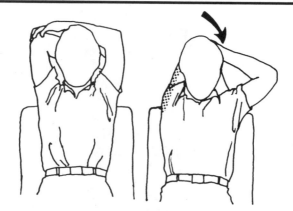

Hold right elbow with left hand, then gently pull elbow
behind head until an easy tension-stretch is felt in shoulder or back of upper arm (triceps). Hold easy stretch for
30 seconds. Do not overstretch. Do both sides.

From a stable, aligned sitting position turn your chin
toward your right shoulder to create a stretch on the right
side of your neck. Hold right stretch tensions for 25-30
seconds. Do each side twice.

If you have a tendency to have a forward head, rounded shoulders, with lower back tension . . . then bring yourself into new alignment. This position, when practiced regularly, will help keep the body fresh with more energy and less tension. This aligned position is done by pulling your chin *in* slightly (not down, not up), with the top of the back of the head being pulled straight up. Think of shoulders back and down. Breathe with the idea that you want the middle of your back to expand outward. Tighten your abdominal muscles as you flatten your lower back into the chair. This is real good to do while driving or sitting to take pressure off of lower back. Practice on this position often as you naturally train your muscles to hold this more alive alignment without conscious effort. Have patience with yourself.

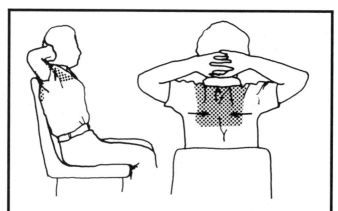

With fingers interlaced behind head, keep elbows straight out to side with upper body in a good aligned position. Now think of pulling your shoulder blades together to create a feeling of tension through upper back and shoulder blades. Hold feeling of releasing tension for 8-10 seconds, then relax. Do several times. This is good to do when shoulders and upper back are tense or tight.

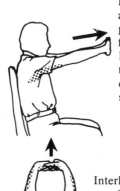

Interlace fingers, then straighten arms out in front of you. The palms should be facing away from you as you do this stretch. Feel stretch in arms and through the upper part of the back (shoulder blades). Hold stretch for 20 seconds. Do at least two times.

Interlace fingers then turn palms upwards above your head as you straighten your arms. Think of elongating your arms as you feel stretch through arms and upper sides of rib cage. Hold for 10 seconds. Hold only stretches that feel releasing. Do three times.

Hold onto your lower leg just below the knee. Gently pull bent leg toward your chest. To isolate a stretch in the side of your upper leg, use the left arm to pull bent leg across and toward the opposite shoulder. Hold for 30 seconds at easy stretch tension. Do both sides.

To stretch the inside of upper leg and hip hold the outside border of the right foot and ankle with the left hand. Your right foot should be resting about mid-thigh. Gently push the inside of your leg (just above your knee, not on the knee) downward to create a stretch in the groin area. Hold for 25-30 seconds. Do both legs.

A stretch for the side of hip, lower and middle of back. Sit
with right leg bent over left leg, then rest elbow of left arm
on the outside of the upper thigh of the right leg. Now
apply some controlled, steady pressure toward the left
with the left elbow. As you do this look over your right
shoulder to get the stretch feeling. Do both sides. Hold for
15 seconds.

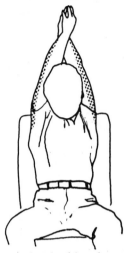

Raise arms overhead with palms touching. Be sure to rotate each arm to outside so each palm is facing to the outside when doing the stretch. To stretch arms, shoulders, and sides of upper back, think of reaching upwards with hands to create a good feeling stretch. Hold for 20 seconds. Do twice.

Hold right lower leg with right hand. With left hand, hold outside border of right foot. Now rotate ankle in a circular motion 20-30 times clockwise, then the same about of times counter-clockwise. This really helps stretch out the ankle joint and relieves tenseness and tiredness.

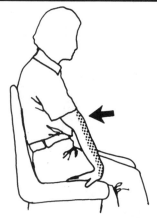

A stretch for the forearm. With the palm of your hand flat, thumb to the outside and fingers pointed backward, slowly lean arm back to get feeling of stretch through forearm. Be sure to keep palm flat, otherwise it will be difficult to create a stretch feeling. Hold for 35-40 seconds. Do both sides. You can stretch both forearms at the same time, if you wish.

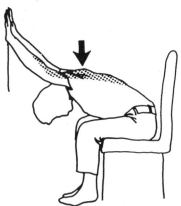

From a sitting position lean forward and hold onto something in front of you. Keep arms as straight as possible as you bend forward at the waist, let chin go toward chest. This will stretch your back, arms, and shoulders. Hold for 40 seconds, then return to an aligned, sitting position.

The foregoing routines are courtesy of Bob and Jean Anderson of Stretching, Inc. Palmer, Colorado 80133. For further information about traveler's stretches, call Stretching, Inc. at 1-800-333-1307.

Metroliner Service
trains routinely reach
speeds of 125 mph.

Courtesy of National
Railroad Passenger Corp.

CHAPTER TEN/
Entertainment On The Train

A side from playing various games at your seat that you brought from home, you can go to the sightseeing lounge or take in a free movie after dinner. Or perhaps you will enjoy the "hospitality hour" that takes place around 4 P.M. in the lounge or bar car , as it is sometimes called. On some trains there are opportunities to join in bingo games, or play a game involving train trivia. The *Amtrak Express* magazine is available free of charge. This traveler's magazine contains a number of general interest articles, as well as feature sections that are entertaining. Long haul trains provide passengers with route guides that tell about points of interest along the way. If the complimentary magazine and the route guide are not in the magazine rack in front of your seat, ask your attendant to get you copies.

From time to time, passengers have been known to play guitars, harmonicas, and have sing-alongs. If the songs are kept in good taste, and the music does not infringe on the comfort of other passengers, train crew personnel will usually not object. I never leave home without several harmonicas in my suitcase. Passengers riding in my car will sometimes discover me relaxing and playing a few familiar melodies while sitting in the Superliner's downstairs vestibule, or at other times, in the crew car.

Notwithstanding the various forms of entertainment already mentioned, in my view, the most enjoyable entertainment on the train is conversation and laughter with other travelers.

CHAPTER ELEVEN/

Special Concerns Of Train Travelers

If You Get Lost On The Train

Sometimes on the longer trains, when passengers leave their seats to wonder around, they lose their way and forget in which car they are seated. You can avoid getting lost on the train by remembering the three or four digit number of your car. At both ends of each car is a three or four digit number at the top of the door on the left, just before you exit the car. That is the number of your car. Disregard the five digit number at the top of each end door. If you get lost, simply tell any uniformed crew member your three or four digit car number, and he or she will direct you back to your car.

Ticket Refunds and Cancellations

What if you buy a ticket from Portland, Oregon, to Chicago, but you decide to end your trip and get off the train in Omaha, Nebraska? Unless there were certain restrictions, you would be entitled to a refund on the unused portion of the ticket. Here's what you do. Several hours before you arrive in Omaha, tell the conductor (or the assistant conductor) that you plan to end your trip in Omaha. Show the conductor your ticket, and ask him or her to issue you a refund claim slip so you can be reimbursed for the unused portion of the ticket. When the refund claim slip is issued, you then mail it, along with the unused portion of your ticket, to

Amtrak Customer Refunds West
Union Station, 210 S. Canal Street
Chicago, IL 60606

If you live east of Ohio and north of Virginia, send your refund claim to

Amtrak Customer Refunds East
30th Street Station, North Tower, 4th Flr.
30th & Market Streets
Philadelphia, PA 19104

Be sure to reproduce a copy of the stub and the refund claim slip for your records, in case you need to follow up. Also, enclose a note tell-ing the customer refunds office that you did not use all your ticket and are requesting a refund. If you purchased your ticket through a travel agency and you are applying for a refund, then you must return the stub and refund claim slip to your travel agency.

Sleeping car tickets can be canceled should you decide not to take the trip. Amtrak requires, however, that such tickets be turned in forty-eight hours before scheduled departure in order to receive full refund. If you cancel a sleeping car ticket less that 48 hours before the scheduled departure, a substantial penalty is imposed. For example, if the total value of the ticket refund was $200, then a penalty of $35 applies; and if the refund came to $500, then a penalty of $110 would be imposed. Therefore, if you plan to turn in your sleeper ticket for cash, do it early. And, as with coach tickets, if you booked through a travel agency then the refund must be processed through it.

Commendation and Complaints

If you have comments about your trip, good or bad, and you wish to share them with Amtrak officials, send them to

Amtrak Customer Relations
60 Massachusetts Ave., NE
Washington, DC 20002

The phone number for Amtrak customer relations is (202) 906-2121. In most cases, however, you will want to write the company so there is documentation supporting your comments. Whenever you write to file a complaint, it is a good idea to forward a copy of your ticket stub. This lets Amtrak know such things as when you traveled and what fare you paid. The Customer Relations office is very efficient, and will do their best to respond quickly and fairly to your letter. If yours is a letter complimenting a certain crew member, they will record the letter and forward it to that crew member. Or, if your letter documents a problem situation, Customer Relations will deal with that as well. In some instances, if Customer Relations feels it is warranted, they will respond to a complaint by issuing a "travel credit" to the passenger(s) involved.

Lost and Found

Always be sure to check around your seat and in the overhead luggage compartment before leaving the train, since it is not easy to retrieve items left behind. If you should accidentally leave something of value on the train, you can contact the Lost and Found at stations near where you got off. First, call the toll-free Amtrak number and ask for the phone number of the station(s) you wish to reach.

Then call the Lost and Found at that station. If you recently detrained and you believe the missing item is still on the train, you can ask the local station keeper to contact the conductor on board about the lost item. Station personnel can contact the train crew by going through the train dispatcher, or by sending a teletype message to the next location where the train is to stop.

Routine Station Stops

Most stops along Amtrak routes are short—about three to five minutes. But roughly every eight to ten hours there are scheduled fuel, water, and trash stops where the train is at the station about fifteen to twenty-five minutes. If the train is running late, however, the conductors will try to reduce the time it takes to service it. Passengers can get off the train during service stops but they should stay fairly near the loading platform, or at least within distance to hear the "all aboard" call. It is your responsibility to be available to re-board at the proper time. If you are not there, the train does not wait. It is most important that passengers heed this information when at stopovers. THE TRAIN WILL LEAVE WITHOUT YOU!

Your Chicago Stopover

If you travel Amtrak very much, there is a good chance you will eventually have a stopover in Chicago. In case you are there for several hours, here are a few things you can do:

❑ Tour part of downtown Chicago. The Sears & Roebuck Tower (tallest building in the world) is just two blocks from the Chicago Union Station. The nationally famous Art Institute of Chicago is ten blocks east at Michigan Avenue and Adams Street. Admission is free on Tuesdays. On other days adults pay $6 and children $3.

❑ Leave your belongings in safe keeping in the station in luggage lockers.

❑ Check in at the First Class Lounge, if you are a sleeper car passenger. This recently renovated facility offers a relaxing atmosphere with complimentary refreshments and a full-time attendant to assist travelers. Ask at the Passenger Services counter for its exact location.

❑ Get information about local transportation at the Passenger Services counter. If you are going to O'Hare Airport, you can take the O'Hare Rapid Transit train which leaves from Clinton and Congress Streets just two blocks south of Union

Station. It's a thirty-five to forty minute ride that costs roughly $1.25.

❑ Enjoy the food from any of a number of restaurants within three or four blocks of the Chicago Union Station. I personally prefer the tasty dishes at Zorba's Greek Restaurant, located four blocks west of Union Station at Halsted and Jackson Streets. If time is critical, there is a McDonalds one block north of Union Station at Clinton and Monroe Streets.

CHAPTER TWELVE /
Questions Passengers Often Ask

"How *ow fast does the train go?"*

The maximum speed of most Amtrak trains is seventy-nine miles per hour. Some trains are permitted to go faster over certain stretches of track, though this is rare. The Metroliner, between New York City and Washington, DC, exceeds 79 miles per hour.

"Why are we stopped here in the middle of nowhere?"

Look out the window on either side. If you see another set of tracks, then it is likely that you're waiting for an oncoming train to pass.[3] If

---

[3] Tracks are leased from other railroad companies, so

it's in the dead of winter and the temperatures are very low, the train may be stopped because an automatic switching mechanism up ahead has frozen and operating crew members are having to activate it manually. Or, it could be that the train is waiting for a folding bridge to go down before it proceeds across the river. There could be any number of other possibilities. I recall the train stopping in the mountains in eastern Oregon to avoid running over a herd of sheep.

"Do train attendants get a chance to sleep?"

Yes, our work schedules usually call for us to sleep from roughly midnight until about 5:50 A.M., and we each have a sleeping berth in the dormitory crew car, or in the sleeper car as space permits. Five hours of sleep per night is about average, although we are required to be up for any major station stop, no matter what time of day or night. Train attendants also have irregular sleeping hours if the train is delayed. Needless to say, if this happens several days in

---

Amtrak trains share the rails with freight trains and are usually given priority over freight trains. But in the Northeast corridor (between Washington D.C. and Boston), Amtrak owns its own tracks and does not have to compete with freight traffic.

a row, passengers may notice a pretty tired train attendant. This is the less glamorous part of what is usually a fun job.

"I'm scheduled to get off the train at around 3 A.M. If I'm asleep, will someone wake me up?"

Yes, you will be awakened by either the conductor, assistant conductor, or the train attendant; and at that hour of the morning, it will most likely be the conductor or assistant. Just be sure that you are in your proper seat under the three-letter destination code and you will definitely be awakened by a crew member.

"May I take a stroll through the sleeping car?"

Yes and no. Yes, if that's the car you are assigned to; and yes, if you are in another car and must go through the sleeper car to get to the diner or the lounge. But you may not walk through the sleeper just to "check it out." Remember, the sleeper car is a bit like a hotel on wheels, and passengers pay handsomely to be able to enjoy their privacy. If you wish to take a look at sleeping car accommodations, ask the attendant for that car to please show you one or two rooms when he or she is not busy.

"Where can I get off the train to make a phone call?"

Ask a crew member where the next service stop is. Trains remain at their service stops for about fifteen to twenty minutes to take on water and fuel. You can make a phone call at that time, but try to keep your conversation brief. It is not recommended that you try to make phone calls at any of the other stops, unless you check with one of the train crew. Also, if the train is behind schedule, then even the longer service stops are often cut short; so stay close enough to hear the "all aboard" call.

"We just boarded the train at 6:15 P.M. Dinner is being served in the diner. May we go there and eat after the conductor takes our tickets?"

Since dinner is served by reservation only, you should ask your train attendant to check with the dining car steward to find out what time is best for you to come to dinner.

"Whom can I contact about upgrading from coach to sleeper car accommodations?"

Contact either the conductor or the assistant conductor. But be warned that there are rarely rooms in the sleeper available to buy once you have boarded the train. Sleeping car rooms are usually booked solid for months in advance, although occasionally, someone with a reservation fails to show up. As Amtrak puts additional sleeper cars into service in the coming years, the scarcity of sleeping berths is likely to be eased.

"There are several empty seats in the next car. May I go sit there?"

Passengers are loaded according to the conductor's loading plan. Check with the conductor or your car attendant. The conductor and train attendant need to know where all passengers are seated so they can insure that they get off at the right station stop. Also, the train crew may have plans to fill empty seats in the next car with passengers that board further along the route.

"May a person flush the toilet when the train is stopped at the station?"

With the older equipment serving routes east of Chicago, the answer is "no." With most Superliner equipment, however, you can flush the toilet anytime, unless a member of the train crew says otherwise. If you are in doubt, ask your attendant.

A surprising number of passengers, when walking through the dining car, ask train crew members the question, "...you eat too?"

If you get the urge to ask this, think a minute. Please, don't ask.

"Can I buy a ticket on board the train?"

The answer is yes, but with qualifications. You can get on a long distance train without a ticket if you board at a scheduled station stop where there is no ticket agent. You would first need to call Amtrak reservations, and they will give you a reservation number to present to the conductor who then sells you a ticket on board the train. On the other hand, if you board the train without a ticket from a station stop where tickets are sold, the conductor will most likely sell you a ticket to the nearest station where tickets are sold. You will then have to get off the train and buy a ticket to your final destination.

So if you are near a ticketing office, purchase your ticket before going on the train. Most conductors are not fond of playing the role of ticket agent, as they have other duties involving the safe and efficient operation of the train that keeps them busy.

Amtrak makes 11 scheduled stops daily while crossing Montana. Powerful locomotives are necessary to get across mountains, and through the meanest weather. Photo Courtesy of Randy Wallenberg of Vashon Island, Washington.

CHAPTER THIRTEEN / *The Train Crew*

Operating Crew

Operating personnel responsible for the safe operation of the train are on duty for roughly seven to nine hours before being replaced by another crew. They include the conductor, one or two assistant conductors, and the engineer and fireman. The conductor is actually in charge of the overall operation of the train. He or she is in regular contact with the dispatcher back on the ground at the control center, and the engineer and fireman up front who run the engine. He or she is the person to see if someone wants to upgrade from coach to sleeper accommodations. Conductors can be recognized by the dark blue slacks and blazer that they generally wear. The sound of the conductor's portable radio often enables one to hear the conductor coming.

Among their many duties, conductors collect tickets from newly arriving passengers, plan what coach cars will carry what passengers, and they insure that passengers get off at their proper stop. Train attendants assist in these tasks. Also, as the one in charge of the train's overall operation, the conductor can decide to put a person who happens to be misbehaving off the train.

The engineer and fireman, who are sometimes referred to in railroad jargon as "hogheads", sit up front in the engine unit. It is possible to hear them talk to the conductors on their portable radios, but you won't see them.

On-Board Service Crew

On-board service crew members include dining car and lounge car workers, train attendants, and the chief of on-board services. If there is a problem in the dining car, contact the dining car steward. In case of a problem in your coach or sleeper car, contact your attendant. You can get to know him or her early on, because your car attendant is in your car most of the time.

Train attendants can be identified by the dark blue slacks and dark blue vest that they wear. They assist passengers in a variety of ways, so passengers should direct most of their questions and requests to the train attendant.

Train attendants keep coach and sleeper cars clean.

It is their job to keep the car clean, help passengers on and off at scheduled stations stops, and they provide a host of other services that make the ride pleasant for passengers. If you're on the train for quite some time, you will likely get to know your attendant better than any other crew member. If a restroom needs some attention, see your attendant. If your overhead reading light doesn't work, see your attendant.

Many attendants will help you decipher your travel itinerary, and using the Amtrak National Timetable, they can assist passengers with helpful tips for planning future travel.

Train attendants stay with the train from the first to last station stop. The one exception to this is with the Sunset Limited, Amtrak's transcontinental train. This train changes on-board service crews in New Orleans.

Since I work as a train attendant, I can confirm that this usually fun-filled job can sometimes turn very demanding. The train is vulnerable to blizzards, flooding, and an occasional derailed freight train that slows traffic in the area. If the train gets off schedule, crew members get off their sleep schedule. As part of the on-board service crew, we are sometimes called on to go the extra mile and pull a smile "out of the hat" to keep our own spirits high, and to reassure impatient passengers who become upset when their carefully laid plans are disrupted.

All on-board service workers are supervised by the Chief of On-Board Services, who is identifiable by his or her gray slacks and dark blue blazer.

CHAPTER FOURTEEN /
Other Sources of Passenger Train Information

If you have a continuing interest in train travel, consider affiliating with a couple passenger train associations. It's a good investment. Their newsletters occasionally include articles about specific Amtrak trains. First, there is The National Association of Railroad Passengers (NARP), 900 Second Street NE, Suite 308, Washington, DC 20002. It publishes a monthly newsletter dealing with rail travel issues of interest to the train traveler. Another long established organization is the National Railway Historical Society (NRHS) at P. O. Box 58153 in Philadelphia, Pennsylvania 19102-8153. They publish a magazine called the *National Railway Bulletin* which is sent periodically to members. The NRHS has chapters across the country in major cities and some of the larger towns, offering members a wealth of information on train travel. Feel free to write and request a complimentary copy of newsletters, along with membership information, from both NARP and NRHS.

Experienced train travelers will tell you that each train tends to have a different "personality." The Coast Starlight is not like The City of New Orleans; The Broadway Limited is not like the Empire Builder, and so on. The "personality" of each of these trains is determined by such things as the train crews who work on board, the passengers who usually take that train, the scenery through which the train passes, the smoothness of the track, and the general atmosphere on board and the physical facilities.

A good source of information about particular trains is a book called *Rail Ventures* by Jack Swanson. It lists the different trains in the Amtrak system and the major points of interest along each route. More recently, John Pitt authored a very informative book, *USA By Rail*. There are also a number of excellent books in print dealing with passenger train history, including Patricia McKissack's, *A Long Hard Journey*, and *Night Trains* by Peter Maiken. Each of these books can be obtained through your local library or from a bookstore.

CHAPTER FIFTEEN /
Tipping

Let it be understood that tipping on the train is not required. In actual practice, however, tipping is common on the train. Let us take a brief historical look at wages and tipping on the train to put the matter in perspective.

By Way Of History

From the time they were first hired (around the end of the Civil War) until about 1900, Pullman porters worked for tips only. Even as late as 1916, they were paid less than $15 per month, a small fraction of the national standard wage rate for that time. Porters and dining car workers alike relied almost exclusively on tips until World War I. They began to organize to press for higher wages, and by the early 1920s, they brought on a young man named A. Philip Randolph to help in their organizing effort. Under Mr. Randolph's leadership, in 1925 the Pullman sleeping car porters formed the first successful African American labor union, the Brotherhood of Sleeping Car Porters. In 1935, this organization was recognized as the sole bargaining agent for some 40,000 railroad workers.

Wages of Pullman porters increased to $78 per month by 1926, and they continued to increase as higher wage contracts were won. Tips, therefore, became less and less important; yet the practice of tipping never completely stopped, mainly because it is a social custom in the United States to tip service workers.

The Practice Today

When passengers eat in the dining car, they usually leave a tip, the same way as patrons in a regular restaurant do. Sleeping car passengers also tip their attendant when they feel satisfactory service is rendered. In my experience, most sleeping car passengers tip from $5 to $10. Some passengers give nothing, while a few give more than $10. Tipping in coach cars is much less frequent, though passengers will, on rare occasions, tip $1 to $5 for especially good service.

It is rare that passengers offer a tip to a conductor, assistant conductor, or chief of onboard services. Persons in these positions do

*A. Philip Randolph. 1890—1977. Leader of the Brother-
hood of Sleeping Car Porters, the first successful African
American labor union. His impact in the labor movement
and civil rights in general is profound. Mr. Randolph is
often said to be the father of the twentieth century civil
rights movement. Photo courtesy of Transportation Com-
munications Union (Amtrak Div.).*

not expect tips, and there is no custom or established practice for it.

Tipping remains a rather uncomfortable issue for some people, but the really important thing is to be personable when you travel by train, and show genuine appreciation for good service. How you do that is ultimately your choice.

Chapter Sixteen / *Passenger Trains In America's Future?*

Is Amtrak on solid financial footing in 1994? Is it likely to be around next year and the year after? In all likelihood, passenger train travel will be part of the American travel scene for quite some time, even though Amtrak (like all large passenger train systems worldwide) depends on Government subsidies to keep it operating.

Some critics say Amtrak needs to operate more efficiently, and that like companies in the private sector, it needs to reduce many positions in middle and upper management. They argue that the federal government is cutting other programs to get control of a runaway national deficit, and that Amtrak cannot afford to continue high overhead costs and long distance trains that don't pay their way. Others have suggested encouraging privately run passenger services—a very unlikely possibility, except in limited situations.

There is a definite need for Amtrak to examine all it's costs, and cut out those that do not contribute meaningfully to high quality service. But one thing is certain: Our country needs more (not fewer) local and long distance trains. As Secretary Morrison mentioned in the Foreword of this book, trains can reduce air pollution and auto traffic congestion, and they can reduce our nation's dependence on foreign oil. We pay a tremendous price for our strong dependence on automobiles. Passenger trains offer a workable option for reducing that dependency.

There was a time in the late 1960s when one could not reliably predict much future for passenger trains in America. But ironically, technological achievements of the last twenty years have made us all aware of some of the questionable results of our technology. As we gain a better understanding of the total price paid as a society for other forms of transportation, we are bound to see train travel as a more acceptable alternative. So don't expect these familiar "iron horses" to go away soon. Let us not forget that passenger trains helped usher in the industrial revolution before the turn of the twentieth century, and they are equally capable of reducing our post-industrial travel problems.

I urge you to take the train often, and share your sentiments about this form of transportation with your representatives in Washington, DC.

INDEX

—A—

Accommodations
  coach 50
  sleeping car 93
  wheelchair 15, 21
African American labor union
  106, 107
Air/Rail travel 41
Air brake 10
Alcoholic beverages 62
"All Aboard America" 40
"AMTRAK Express" 81
AMTRAK National Timetable
  102
AMTRAK, future of 109
Anderson, Bob 79
Anderson, Jean 79
Animals 26
Art Institute of Chicago 88
Attendants, services 20, 21

—B—

Baby changing platform 14
Baggage 19, 24
Baltimore and Ohio 5
Bicycles 24
Blankets 33, 67
Boarding the train 54
Bombardier Corporation 12
Booking 30
  sleeping cars 49, 50
Breakfast 60
Broadway limited 104

Brotherhood of Sleeping Car
  Porters 106
Bunk cars 7

—C—

Cancellations 84
Car attendant 15, 17, 19, 62, 67
Car number 83
Car porters 106
Central Pacific 9
Checked baggage 55, 56
Checking baggage 24, 25
Chicago 47, 48
  stopover 87
  Union Station 88, 89
Chief of On-Board Services 15,
  100, 102
Children's fares 41
City of New Orleans 104
Claim check 25
Coach
  accommodations 50
  passengers 62
  reservations 53
  sleeping on 67
  ticket 55
  tipping 106
Coach car 13
Coast Starlight 50, 104
Commendations 85, 86
Common carriers 68
Complaints 85, 86
Conductor 15, 17, 95, 96, 99
Connecting time 56
Connections 32

Crew members 19, 83, 100
Customer Relations 85, 86
Deluxe rooms 3, 18
Dining car 13, 20, 59, 61, 94
    tipping 106
"Disabled" fares 40
Discount fares 37
Dogs 26

–E–

Eating
    coach 62
    diner 59
Economy rooms 3, 16, 17, 18
Emancipation Proclamation 8
Empire Builder 104
Engineer 100
Family room 18
Fares 37, 39
    air/rail 41
    "All Aboard America" 40
    children's 41
    "disabled" 40
    discount 37
    group travel 47
    military 40
    off-peak 39
    senior 40
    USA Railpass 44

–F–

Fireman 100
First-class lounge 88
Food
    fresh 62, 63
    private 62

–G–

Glacier National Park 67
Great American Vacations 30

Group travel 47

–H–

Handwritten tickets 31
Hearing-impaired services 22,
    81
Hoghead 100
Hospitality hour 3
Hotel on Wheels 93

–I–

Ice 62
Interstate commerce 5
Iron horse 5, 110

–J–

Jarvis, John B. 5

–K–

King Street Station 56
Kosher 61

–L–

Light, overhead 100
Lost passenger 83
Lost and Found 86
Lounge, (in Chicago) 88
Lounge car 13, 20, 61, 67, 69, 81
Lowfat meals 61
Luggage lockers 88

–M–

Maiken, Peter 104
Map—"All Aboard America"
    zones 43
Map—AMTRAK National Sys-
    tem 44, 45
McDonald's 89

McKissack, Patricia and Floyd 8
Meal service 19
Meal voucher 19
Meals 18
    breakfast 60
    dinner 61
    lunch 61
    prices 60, 61
    selection 60
    special 22, 61
Metroliner 91
Military fares 40
Mobility impaired 14
Movie 81
Musical instruments 82

–N–

National Association of Railroad Passengers 103, 104
National Railway Bulletin 103
National Railroad Passenger Corp. 4, 11
National Railway Historical Society 103, 104
Neck pillow 67
Northeast corridor 92

–O–

O'Hare Rapid Transit 88
Off-peak season 17
Operating crew 99

–P–

Pacific Railroad Act 9
Packing 25
Passenger comments 85, 86
Passenger trains 6, 68
Phone calls 94
Phone numbers

TDD 22
    customer relations 86
    reservations 18
    Great America Vacations 18
Pillows 15, 33, 67
Pioneer, The 7, 10
Porters 105
Private garden 63
Profile screen 47
Promontory, Utah 9
Pullman porters 9, 105
Pullman Sleeping Car Co. 7, 8, 9, 11
Pullman, George M. 7, 8
Rail travel history 5
Refund claim slip 84
Refunds 84
Reinhardt, Richard 6
Reservations 14, 49
    phone number 18
    reconfirming 31
Restrooms 17, 21, 100

–S–

Scheduled stops 87
Sears and Roebuck Tower 88
Seat check 55
Seeing eye dogs 26
Senior citizens 20
    fares 40
Sightseeing lounge 2, 20
Sing-a-long 82
Skis 24
Sleeper cars 2, 7, 13, 18, 85, 93, 94, 95
    booking 30, 49, 50
    luggage 24
    reconfirming 30
    services 19

Sleeping accommodations 50,
  51, 62, 65
Sleeping
  coach cars 67
  sleeper cars 66
Slumber coach 18
Smoking 68
Special seating section 14, 23
Special assistance 31
Special bedroom 18
Special needs 20
  bathroom 21
  bedroom 21
Special meals 22, 61
Speed 91
Sprouting plants 63
Station personnel 87
Station stops 87
Stations
  Green River, WY 52
  King Street (Seattle, WA) 56
  Olympia-Lacey, WA 57
  Salem, OR 52
Stevens, John 5
Steward (dining car) 19, 94
Stretching 65, 66
Sunset Limited 102
Superliner II 12
Superliner bedroom 27
Superliner 14
TDD phone number 22
Ticket
  cancellations 84
  purchase 96
  refunds 84

stub 84
upgrading 94

–T–

Time zones 6
Tipping 105, 106
Toilet, flushing 17, 95
Toll-free reservation number 53
Train dispatcher 87
Train speed 91
Train attendants 99-102
  eat 95, 96
  sleep 92
Travel group 2
Travel agent 18, 29, 85
Travel credit 86
Travelers' stretches 69-79

–U–

Union Pacific 9
Unmanned stations 25
USA Railpass 44

–V–

Voucher (meal) 19

–W–

Wages, Pullman porters 105,
  106
Wheelchair accommodations 15
World War II 10

–Z–

Zorba's Greek Restaurant 89

Neck Nest
(Neck Pillow)

This inflatable neck pillow (made of velour) supports the head and neck for more comfortable rest on the train, car, airplane, or even watching T.V. It has a safety valve, and comes with a carrying pouch.

Bucky™ U-Travel
(Neck Pillow)

This incredibly comfortable pillow is filled with light, movable, soothing buckwheat hulls that conform to the perfect shape to cradle your head and neck for relaxed snoozing on the train and elsewhere. It has a beautiful soft fleece cover that zips off for easy washing, and it comes with a carrying case.

TO ORDER:Copy this form and mail it to:

Apollo Publishing Co.
P.O. Box 1937
Port Orchard, WA 98366-0805

Or Call 1-800-308-5273 to place an order

Date: _____

☐ Send Me_____ copies of the book AMTRAKing at $8.95 per copy, and $3 for postage and handling. (No additional postage and handling fee when ordering more than one book).

☐ Send me_____ Neck Nest brand neck pillow(s) at $7.95 each plus $3 postage & handling.

☐ Send me_____ Bucky brand neck pillow(s) at $21.95 each and $3 postage & handling.

(Note: No additional postage and handling fee when ordering more than one neck pillow).

*Name*_____

*Address*_____

*City/State/Zip*_____

☐ Enclosed is a check or money order in the amount of $_____ (made out to Apollo Publishing Co.)

Charge my: ☐ Mastercard   ☐ Visa

Card #_____Exp. Date_____

Signature_____